# CRUSH YOUR GOALS!

## The Field Guide

29 Worksheets and Self Assessments
for Maximizing Your Success

# CRUSH YOUR GOALS!™

**THE FIELD GUIDE**

*29 Worksheets and Self Assessments for Maximizing Your Success*

## AUSTIN BOLLINGER

*Founder of DailyNewYears.com*

Copyright © 2020 B&B Media, L.L.C.

Published in the United States by Daily New Year's, a division of B&B Media, L.L.C., Missouri.

All rights reserved.

No part of this publication may be reproduced, distributed, or transmitted in any form or by any means, including photocopying, recording, or other electronic or mechanical methods, without the prior written permission of the publisher, except in the case of brief quotations embodied in critical reviews and certain other noncommercial uses permitted by copyright law.

Although the author and publisher have made every effort to ensure that the information in this book was correct at press time, the author and publisher do not assume and hereby disclaim any liability to any party for any loss, damage, or disruption caused by errors or omissions, whether such errors or omissions result from negligence, accident, or any other cause.

Adherence to all applicable laws and regulations, including international, federal, state, and local governing professional licensing, business practices, advertising, and all other aspects of doing business in the US, Canada, or any other jurisdiction is the sole responsibility of the reader and consumer.

Neither the author nor the publisher assumes any responsibility or liability whatsoever on behalf of the consumer or reader of this material. Any perceived slight of any individual or organization is purely unintentional.

The resources in this book are provided for informational purposes only and should not be used to replace the specialized training and professional judgment of a health care or mental health care professional.

Neither the author nor the publisher can be held responsible for the use of the information provided within this book. Please always consult a trained professional before making any decision regarding treatment of yourself or others.

ISBN 978-1-7345507-5-7

Categories: 1. Personal Success 2. Personal Transformation 3. Success

Printed in the United States of America

Cover Design by Austin Bollinger

First Edition

## Downloading Extra Worksheets

As you use the resources within this field guide, you may wish to have additional copies of the worksheets or assessments. That's awesome! I hope you find so much value here that you continue using the worksheets and resources for years to come.

Please visit www.crushyourgoalsbook.com/resources for full access to all of the worksheets found within this book. They're completely free.

# Contents

## Section 1: Cultivating a Goal Getter's Mindset .................. 11

1. Find and Embrace Your Why .................................................. 13
2. Overcome the Six Fears of Goal Setting ............................ 23
3. How to Build Rock-Solid Self-Confidence ........................ 53
4. Develop a Goal Getter's Mindset ........................................ 63

## Section 2: Getting Started with Goal Setting ..................... 73

5. The FOCUSED Framework .................................................... 75
6. Four Universal Goals to Start Setting Today ................... 87
7. Prioritize Like a Pro & Crush Your Goals in Record Time ..... 99
8. The Best Tools for Tracking Your Goals ........................... 113

## Section 3: Establishing a System for Success ......................... 121

**9.** Assemble a Support Team ........................................................ 123

**10.** The Four Cs of High-Performance Goal Setting ....................... 135

**11.** Develop a Daily, Success-Driven Routine .......................... 145

**12.** Build Momentum Using the Domino Effect ............................. 153

## Section 4: Dealing with Difficulties .............................................. 161

**13.** How to Stay Motivated ............................................................ 163

**14.** Five Tips for Overcoming Obstacles ................................... 175

**15.** Moving Beyond Failure ........................................................... 185

**16.** Take Action Today! ................................................................. 195

## SECTION 1

# CULTIVATING A GOAL GETTER'S MINDSET

# Find and Embrace Your Why

*"If you get a big enough 'why' you can do anything."*
– Tony Robbins

*Crush Your Goals!*

**CHAPTER NOTES**

Following the previous chapter, how are you feeling? What thoughts are running through your mind? Jot them down here for later reference.

## *Discover and Embrace Your Why*

***Crush Your Goals!***

## *Discover and Embrace Your Why*

**WORKSHEET**

## *Discover and Embrace Your Why*

⑦ Do you believe that if you have a strong enough *why*, you can do anything? Why or why not?

_____
_____
_____
_____
_____

⑦ Do you agree that your *why* is one of the most important factors to your goal-setting success—your foundation? Why or why not?

_____
_____
_____
_____
_____
_____

⑦ Thinking back over your life, can you recall a goal that you pursued with a passionate vigor—a goal that seemed to be driving you forward? Describe it here:

_____
_____
_____
_____

*Discover and Embrace Your Why*

⑦ **How was that goal different from the goals you've been setting more recently?**

☐ **Write one of your newer goals here:**

⑦ **Simon Sinek says, "Your *why* is the purpose, cause or belief that inspires you." *Why* do you want to achieve the goal above?**

Don't simply accept the first, surface-level *why* that comes to you. Don't be afraid to dig deep and form an emotional connection with the goal.

*Crush Your Goals!*

⑦ **Is your *why* meaningful? Does it excite and inspire you? Will your *why* keep driving you forward? Why or why not?**

Is the goal wrong, or is the timing wrong? Journal your thoughts here and be 100% honest with yourself. It's okay to drop a goal or save it for later. We need to be sure that our *whys* are strong enough to continue propelling us forward.

_____

_____

_____

_____

_____

_____

_____

⑦ **Are you prone to saying yes to everything that comes your way, whether you want to do it or not? If so, how does that affect your goals, your attitude, and your spirit?**

_____

_____

_____

_____

_____

_____

_____

⑦ **Using your *why* as a filter, how will you address new opportunities or tasks that may threaten to derail your goal? Craft a strategy here:**

_____

_____

_____

*Discover and Embrace Your Why*

? **Off the top of your head, what are some things you can say "no" to right away?**

1. 
2. 
3. 
4. 
5. 

? **Knowing what you know now, are you okay with saying "no" to these opportunities as a way to defend your goal or goals? Why or why not?**

? **Do you feel like you now have a solid foundation for moving forward with the rest of this book? Why or why not?**

# Overcome the Six Fears of Goal Setting

*"Inaction breeds doubt and fear. Action breeds confidence and courage. If you want to conquer fear, do not sit home and think about it. Go out and get busy."*

– Dale Carnegie

## CHAPTER NOTES

Following the previous chapter, how are you feeling? What thoughts are running through your mind? Jot them down here for later reference.

_____
_____
_____
_____
_____
_____
_____
_____
_____
_____
_____
_____
_____
_____
_____
_____
_____
_____
_____
_____
_____

## *Overcome the Six Fears of Goal Setting*

## *Crush Your Goals!*

**Overcome the Six Fears of Goal Setting**

*Crush Your Goals!*

**WORKSHEET**

## *Overcoming the 6 Fears of Goal Setting*

⊙ **Of the Six Fears, which ones did you resonate with the most? Which stood out to you?**

Select all that apply and then proceed to the following worksheets.

☐ **Fear of Loss**
When you fear loss, you may be afraid that your potential goals are going to cost you something that you may be unwilling to lose.

☐ **Fear of Judgment and Rejection**
When you fear rejection, your fear what others may think of you, in failure and success. This gives people the power to make you feel guilty for wanting something more.

☐ **Fear of Discontent**
When you fear discontent, you worry that your ambitions might make you seem ungrateful or not thankful for your current place in life.

☐ **Fear of the Unknown**
When you fear the unknown, you worry about choosing the wrong path or you may fear what your current path will someday mean for your life.

☐ **Fear of Failure**
When you fear failure, you avoid setting goals because it's easier to stay where you are than it is to gamble on something new, even if the new thing is far better than what you have.

☐ **Fear of Success**
When you fear success, you worry that you'll be ill-equipped to handle the new levels you've reached in life. To you, greater success equals larger responsibility and you're unsure of your ability to perform at a higher level.

**WORKSHEET**

## *Overcoming the Fear of Loss*

⓪ **List a couple goals that you've set for yourself in the past that you have failed to achieve for some unknown reason. Or, list a few goals you've wanted to pursue, but haven't for some unknown reason.**

For example, "I've always wanted to get in shape, but I just can't seem to get started." Or, "I've always wanted to start my own business, but I've never pulled the trigger."

_____

_____

_____

_____

_____

⓪ **For each of the goals above, can you identify something that you were afraid to lose or give up? Are you afraid to lose friends, a particular idea or belief, your way of life, your belongings, or something else?**

For example, some people resist setting weight-loss goals because they believe it might cause them to lose their favorite foods. Others refrain from pursuing side-hustles because they fear it might cost them all of their free time.

_____

_____

_____

_____

_____

⓪ **Many times, FEAR is actually False Expectations Appearing Real. Will your potential goals truly cause you to lose something in reality? Why or why not?**

For example, "Starting my side business is going to cause me to lose some free time. I'll either have to work weekends, nights, or early mornings to get it started."

## *Overcome the Six Fears of Goal Setting*

Or, "getting in shape seems like it's going to cost me all of my favorite foods, but depending on the diet I choose, that may not be entirely true."

⑦ **If your new goals will actually cost you something, will it be worth it? Is what you're gaining going to be better than what you're losing? Why or why not?**

For example, "Giving up my mornings and weekends to start my side hustle may cost me some freedom initially, but over time, it will actually give me more freedom, and that's worth losing a few mornings and some sleep here and there."

⑦ **If the new goals you have in mind are in fact going to cost you something that you're unwilling to lose, are you okay with giving up the goal? Why or why not?**

**WORKSHEET**

## *Overcoming the Fear of Rejection*

⑦ **Of all the people in your life, who are you afraid will ridicule, reject, or judge you? If you can, list them out by name and how you think they'll judge you.**

For example, "I'm afraid my parents won't approve of my skipping college to pursue the career I've chosen for myself. College isn't necessary, but they won't see it that way and I'm worried they will pressure me into doing it their way."

_____

_____

_____

_____

_____

_____

_____

⑦ **At the end of the day, do you truly value the opinions of the people above?**

Cross out the people above whose opinions you do not truly value. You're not crossing them out of your life; you're just working towards freeing yourself of their opinions. Then, circle the names above of those whose opinions that do matter to you.

⑦ **What are some of your thoughts following the selections you made above?**

For example, "I love and respect my parents, but I can't allow their believes to prevent me from pursuing the career that I'm passionate about. I value their opinions, so I need to talk to them about my goals."

_____

_____

_____

## *Overcome the Six Fears of Goal Setting*

_____
_____
_____
_____
_____
_____
_____

**⑦ To overcome your fear of rejection, you have to face it head on. For this exercise, you need to meet with each of the people you value and explain your goals to them and why you want to achieve them. Let them know you care about them and that you value their support.**

For example, you might sit down with your parents and explain how student debt is one of the fastest and largest types of debt in the world and that hands-on experience is more important to your chosen profession than a formal education. You could show them examples and success stories from people who have gone before you, as well as your plan to succeed.

Approach these conversations with love and understanding. Don't be combative. Understand that it may take time for your friends and family to see your point of view. If they respond poorly, give them time and then approach them again later, but don't allow their lack of support weaken your resolve.

If they still don't support you after several conversations, let them know your intentions. Don't let the fear of ridicule or rejection hold you back from your goals.

**👉 Using the following lines, list out the people you circled on the previous page and then use this list to track your one-on-one conversations.**

As you meet with the people you value, check them off the list.

☐ _____
☐ _____
☐ _____
☐ _____
☐ _____

***Crush Your Goals!***

❓ **Following your one-on-one conversations, how are you feeling? Did the conversations go well, or did they go poorly?**

If any of them went poorly, how will you move forward without worrying about rejection or judgment?

_____
_____
_____
_____
_____
_____
_____
_____
_____

↪ **For the people you crossed out on the previous page—the ones whose opinions you don't value—prepare yourself mentally for their negative feedback, but move forward in spite of it.**

If you try and fail, they may laugh. That's okay! Remember, you don't value their opinion, right?

Understand that it's most often the people too afraid to try something new who laugh at those who have the courage to try new things. Don't resent them for their lack of support or their negative comments. More than likely, they have a fear of failure or a fear of the unknown themselves. Deep down, they may wish they were brave enough to take a risk and try something new.

Whether you know it or not, when you push forward with your dreams in spite of ridicule or judgment, you become an inspiration to those too afraid to try.

## *Overcome the Six Fears of Goal Setting*

⑦ **Finally, what will you do when faced with ridicule, rejection, or judgment? What's your plan for overcoming these reactions? What will you do when you encounter this behavior?**

Use the following lines to write out your plan. How will you respond? What will you say? What will you do?

___
___
___
___
___
___
___
___
___

⑦ **Following this chapter and the exercises, do you feel you're better equipped to move forward with your goals? Are you free from the fear of rejection? Why or why not?**

___
___
___
___
___
___
___
___

**WORKSHEET**

## *Overcoming the Fear of Discontent*

The Fear of Discontent is the fear of constantly wanting more in life and being ungrateful for what you have, but improvement is very much a part of life.

As a baby, you were most likely not content with crawling around on the floor—instead, you learned to walk, and then you learned to run. You leveled up. For most of us, that was an unconscious decision. Throughout your life there have been countless places where discontent has caused you to push for more. Somewhere along the way, maybe you stopped pushing. Let's find out why.

> **Think about out some of the ways you've intentionally leveled throughout your life and list them below. Why were those positive experiences?**
>
> For example, "I decided to pursue a college degree because I wasn't content with the options a high school diploma gave me. There's absolutely nothing wrong with a high school diploma, but I wanted a career in a competitive industry. I wouldn't have the career I have today had I not pursued my goal of obtaining my four-year degree."

_____
_____
_____
_____
_____
_____
_____
_____
_____

## Overcome the Six Fears of Goal Setting

⑦ After listing out some of your life experiences that caused you to level up, reflect on where you might be had you settled for "good enough." What if you had been content?

_____
_____
_____
_____
_____
_____
_____
_____
_____

⑦ Throughout life you've been leveling up; it's how you got to where you are today. When do you think you stopped pushing yourself? Why do you think that is?

_____
_____
_____
_____
_____
_____
_____
_____
_____

? **If you're afraid of feeling discontent or ungrateful for your life, it helps to focus on how your goals will help you grow. What areas of life do you hope to grow in? How will setting goals help you grow in those areas?**

? **If you were to change nothing about your life for the next 20 years, do you think you would be okay with how your life turned out? Would you be happy with yourself?**

There's nothing wrong with being grateful for your life as it is today, but living life to the fullest means growing as a person. Would you be content in 20 years if you didn't grow beyond today?

## Overcome the Six Fears of Goal Setting

⑦ **What are some areas in your life that you're not content with today? How can you improve in those areas while still being grateful for what you have?**

For example, you might want to deepen your relationships or your spirituality because you're discontent with your connections to the people around you. Maybe you want to go back to school or seek a promotion because you're discontent with your career. Perhaps you want to travel and experience more of the world because you're discontent with your world view.

_____
_____
_____
_____
_____
_____
_____
_____

⑦ **Following this chapter and the exercises, do you feel better equipped to give yourself permission to be okay with discontent as a means to allow yourself to grow? Why or why not?**

_____
_____
_____
_____
_____
_____
_____
_____

**WORKSHEET**

## *Overcoming the Fear of the Unknown*

⑦ **Which aspect of the unknown do you fear the most: not knowing what you want in life, picking the correct path (of many) for your life, or both? Why?**

_____
_____
_____

⑦ **Based on the lessons in this chapter, what advice would you give a friend suffering from the same fear?**

_____
_____
_____
_____
_____

⑦ **If you're unsure of which path to choose for your life, could you make a list of each option and then list the pros and cons of each?**

For example, "I'm torn between staying at my job, pursuing a new job, or starting my own business, and I'm not sure which option is the best."

**1.** _____

Pros                                    Cons

_____          _____
_____          _____

## Overcome the Six Fears of Goal Setting

**2.** _____

Pros

Cons

**3.** _____

Pros

Cons

**4.** _____

Pros

Cons

### ⑦ Using your new pros and cons list, which path for your life are you most excited about right now? Why?

Trust your gut and your feelings. Which option gives you a surge of excitement and why?

*Crush Your Goals!*

⑦ **If your fear of the unknown leaves you unsure of what you want in life, use the space below to practice Blue-Sky Thinking.**

Imagine you had absolutely no limits. You could do anything, be anything, and go anywhere you wanted. What would you do? Where would you go? What would your life look like as a whole? Try journaling your vision of your life here and give yourself some time to dream. Be patient; this isn't an easy exercise, but it will help; I promise.

_____
_____
_____
_____
_____
_____
_____
_____
_____
_____
_____
_____
_____
_____
_____

⑦ **Using either the results from the previous page or your vision from the Blue-Sky Thinking exercise, what immediate next steps can you take to put one of the two plans in motion today?**

1. _____
2. _____
3. _____

## *Overcome the Six Fears of Goal Setting*

**4.** _____

**5.** _____

**6.** _____

**7.** _____

**8.** _____

⑦ **Knowing that the future can never be known, do you agree that taking action and choosing any path is better than choosing no path? Why or why not?**

> Will you sit in the passenger seat and let life take you wherever it wants, or will you take the wheel, set some goals, and choose your own path?

_____

_____

_____

_____

_____

_____

_____

⑦ **Following this chapter and the exercises, do you feel better equipped to move forward into the unknown? Why or why not?**

_____

_____

_____

_____

_____

_____

**WORKSHEET**

## *Overcoming the Fear of Failure*

⑦ Overcoming the fear of failure often means accepting the possibility of failure as an outcome as well as your ability to persevere. What are some ways you've failed in the past? How did you overcome those situations?

_____
_____
_____
_____
_____

⑦ Reflect on one of your past failures that helped you grow the most. How did a failure in your life make you stronger, better, or smarter?

_____
_____
_____
_____
_____

⑦ Often times, ignoring your fears gives power to them. Acknowledging them, however, can help you in overcoming them. Can you describe one of the fears you're facing right now? What are you afraid of?

_____
_____
_____

## Overcome the Six Fears of Goal Setting

_____
_____
_____

⑦ **What are the symptoms of your fear? Some examples include: procrastination, anxiety, depression, lack of self confidence, perfectionism, avoidance, negative self-talk, apathy, or feeling stuck or overwhelmed.**

1. _____
2. _____
3. _____
4. _____
5. _____
6. _____

⑦ **What purpose do these symptoms serve? Are they helping you, or hurting you? What are you trying to avoid?**

Dig deep. If you're unsure of what you're afraid of, analyzing your symptoms can help uncover the truth about your fears and allow you to craft a plan for overcoming your fears.

_____
_____
_____
_____
_____
_____
_____
_____

*Crush Your Goals!*

⑦ **Do you agree that not trying at all is more of a failure than trying and missing the mark? Why or why not?**

_____
_____
_____
_____
_____
_____

⑦ **Think about one of your past failures. How might you learn a lesson from that failure so that you might redefine it as a success?**

_____
_____
_____
_____
_____
_____

⑦ **Fear Setting is the practice of writing down your biggest fear and then crafting a plan for overcoming it. If the biggest fear you have surrounding your goals were to come true today, how would you overcome it?**

Most people fear the what-ifs surrounding a failure, but when forced to deal with the situation, they often persevere and overcome it. For example, many people fear losing their job, but when it happens, they often rebound and find a new, better job in a short amount of time.

Write down a step-by-step plan for overcoming the worst-case scenario surrounding your goals.

**1.** _____

**2.** _____

**3.** _____

**Overcome the Six Fears of Goal Setting**

4. _____
5. _____
6. _____
7. _____
8. _____
9. _____
10. _____

⑦ **Following the Fear Setting exercise, do you feel better equipped to overcome the potential failure you're facing? Why or why not?**

_____
_____
_____
_____
_____

⑦ **Following this chapter and the exercises, do you feel better equipped to face your fears head-on? Why or why not? If not, will you move forward with courage and face them anyway?**

_____
_____
_____
_____
_____
_____

**WORKSHEET**

## *Overcoming the Fear of Success*

⑦ **What does achieving your goals mean for your future? In other words, if you succeed in crushing all of your biggest goals, what does life look like for you?**

Are you traveling the world, living in a mansion, driving around in a Lamborghini, running a Fortune 500 company, or something else? Dig deep and dream big here. Don't be afraid to write down what true success could mean for your future.

_____
_____
_____
_____
_____

⑦ **Now, on a scale of 1-10, how much does achieving that future of success scare you?**

With 1 being "It's very scary!" and 10 being "I'm not scared at all! I can't wait!"

| 1 | 2 | 3 | 4 | 5 | 6 | 7 | 8 | 9 | 10 |
|---|---|---|---|---|---|---|---|---|----|

⑦ **Assuming you ranked closer to the lower end of the scale, why do you think that is? If most of us want to succeed, why would we be afraid of success?**

_____
_____
_____
_____
_____

## *Overcome the Six Fears of Goal Setting*

⑦ Many times, achieving success means leaving our current zone of comfort. Describe your current comfort zone. Do you want to leave it? Why or why not?

_____
_____
_____
_____
_____

⑦ Achieving success in our goals means that our lives may change in many ways and we will have to leave our comfort zone behind. In what ways will your life change if you achieve success?

_____
_____
_____
_____
_____

⑦ Are you ready for the big changes you detailed above? Why or why not?

_____
_____
_____
_____
_____
_____

***Overcome the Six Fears of Goal Setting***

- ⑦ Deep down, many of us suffer from Gay Hendricks's Upper Limit Problem, or the belief that we cannot attain a higher level of success, or that if we do attain it, we'll be ill-equipped to handle it. Do you think you suffer from this mindset? Why or why not?

- ⑦ Reflecting on your past, has the Upper Limit Problem ever surfaced and caused you to sabotage your own success? How so?

- ⑦ Throughout your life there have been countless times where you've leveled up. Every time you advanced a grade in school, got promoted, learned a new skill, and so on are all times where you've achieved success and leveled up in your life. List 10 of your biggest successes that have caused you to level up in your life.

1. 
2. 
3.

## Overcome the Six Fears of Goal Setting

4. _____
5. _____
6. _____
7. _____
8. _____
9. _____
10. _____

❓ **Reflecting on your successes above, how did you deal with your newfound success? Did life get a little harder before it got easier again? How did you manage it? Do you think you could deal with your future success in the same way?**

_____
_____
_____
_____
_____
_____

❓ **Following this chapter and the exercises, do you feel better equipped to move forward into the unknown? Why or why not?**

_____
_____
_____
_____
_____
_____

# How to Build Rock-Solid Self-Confidence

*"Each time we face our fear, we gain strength, courage and confidence in the doing."*

– Theodore Roosevelt

**CHAPTER NOTES**

Following the previous chapter, how are you feeling? What thoughts are running through your mind? Jot them down here for later reference.

## How to Build Rock-Solid Self-Confidence

*Crush Your Goals!*

## How to Build Rock-Solid Self-Confidence

**WORKSHEET**

# Building Rock-Solid Self-Confidence

⑦ **How would you rate your self-confidence in the area of goal setting?**

1 being "I doubt I'm going to achieve this goal" and 10 being "I have an excellent chance of crushing this goal."

| 1 | 2 | 3 | 4 | 5 | 6 | 7 | 8 | 9 | 10 |

⑦ **How would you rate your self-discipline?**

1 being "I'm not at all disciplined" and 10 being "I don't think I could be more disciplined if I tried."

| 1 | 2 | 3 | 4 | 5 | 6 | 7 | 8 | 9 | 10 |

⑦ **How would you rate your self-esteem?**

1 being "I don't feel very good about myself or my accomplishments" and 10 being "I have really good self-esteem and I'm proud of my accomplishments."

| 1 | 2 | 3 | 4 | 5 | 6 | 7 | 8 | 9 | 10 |

⑦ **Given the lessons in this chapter, would you agree that self-discipline, self-confidence, and self-esteem are closely related? Why or why not?**

_____
_____
_____
_____
_____
_____

*How to Build Rock-Solid Self-Confidence*

⑦ **As you seek to build your self-confidence and crush your goals, what are some ways you can improve your own self-discipline?**

Could you build a routine around your goals, get an accountability partner, etc? More on these topics in chapters 9, 10, and 11 if you would like to read more.

_____

_____

_____

_____

_____

_____

_____

_____

_____

⑦ **When you prioritize yourself, you begin to feel more important and valuable. What are some ways you can begin to prioritize your own goals? If you're a caretaker, how can you begin to balance your priorities with the expectations of those depending on you?**

_____

_____

_____

_____

_____

_____

_____

_____

*Crush Your Goals!*

⑦ Think about the past 15-30 days. How many things did you say yes to when you really wanted to say no? Did those things take time away from your own goals? How did that make you feel?

_____
_____
_____
_____
_____

⑦ How can you begin to improve upon your ability to say no to things that conflict with your own goals?

_____
_____
_____
_____
_____

⑦ What are some ways you can use the Confidence/Competence loop to your advantage? In the coming weeks and months, what are some ways you can learn more about your active goals? Do you think this will help you feel more confident? Why or why not?

_____
_____
_____
_____
_____

## How to Build Rock-Solid Self-Confidence

⑦ When we feel inadequate, we don't feel good enough. One of the biggest reasons people don't set goals is due to not feeling good enough to achieve them. What would you tell a friend who was suffering from this problem?

⑦ If you're lacking self-confidence, you might find yourself resisting taking action towards your goals. To give yourself a boost, what 3-5 things can you do this week to put your goals in motion? How can you take Massive Action?

# Develop a Goal Getter's Mindset

*"It's hard to beat a person who never gives up."*

– Babe Ruth

## CHAPTER NOTES

Following the previous chapter, how are you feeling? What thoughts are running through your mind? Jot them down here for later reference.

*Develop a Goal Getter's Mindset*

## Crush Your Goals!

## Develop a Goal Getter's Mindset

*Crush Your Goals!*

**WORKSHEET**

# *Developing a Goal Getter's Mindset*

**⑦ For the following nine mindsets, evaluate your current ability to embrace and practice the mindset.**

1 being "I'm really struggling with this one" and 10 being "I believe and live this mindset everyday."

**⑦ Then, try to describe an experience when you either embraced and embodied the mindset, or an experience when you failed to practice the mindset.**

By reflecting on a time when you failed to practice a mindset, you can learn when you might need to call upon it in the future. For example, after reflecting on all the times that perfectionism caused me to procrastinate, quit, or extend my timelines unnecessarily, I now actively remind myself to avoid this trap while engaging in a project.

☐ **1. The Better Every Day Mindset**

| 1 | 2 | 3 | 4 | 5 | 6 | 7 | 8 | 9 | 10 |
|---|---|---|---|---|---|---|---|---|----|

_____
_____
_____
_____
_____

☐ **2. The Lifelong Learner Mindset**

| 1 | 2 | 3 | 4 | 5 | 6 | 7 | 8 | 9 | 10 |
|---|---|---|---|---|---|---|---|---|----|

_____
_____
_____
_____
_____

*Develop a Goal Getter's Mindset*

☐ **3. The Positivity and Perseverance Mindset**

| 1 | 2 | 3 | 4 | 5 | 6 | 7 | 8 | 9 | 10 |
|---|---|---|---|---|---|---|---|---|----|

_____
_____
_____
_____
_____
_____

☐ **4. The Responsibility Mindset**

| 1 | 2 | 3 | 4 | 5 | 6 | 7 | 8 | 9 | 10 |
|---|---|---|---|---|---|---|---|---|----|

_____
_____
_____
_____
_____
_____

☐ **5. The Self Belief Mindset**

| 1 | 2 | 3 | 4 | 5 | 6 | 7 | 8 | 9 | 10 |
|---|---|---|---|---|---|---|---|---|----|

_____
_____
_____
_____
_____
_____

☐ **6. The Act As if Mindset**

| 1 | 2 | 3 | 4 | 5 | 6 | 7 | 8 | 9 | 10 |

_____
_____
_____
_____

☐ **7. The You Are What You Eat Mindset**

| 1 | 2 | 3 | 4 | 5 | 6 | 7 | 8 | 9 | 10 |

_____
_____
_____
_____

☐ **8. The Unlimited Potential Mindset**

| 1 | 2 | 3 | 4 | 5 | 6 | 7 | 8 | 9 | 10 |

_____
_____
_____
_____

☐ **9. The GETMO Mindset**

| 1 | 2 | 3 | 4 | 5 | 6 | 7 | 8 | 9 | 10 |

***Develop a Goal Getter's Mindset***

⑦ **Of the nine mindsets, which one do you practice most often? Which one comes easiest to you and why?**

⑦ **Which one gives you the most trouble? Why?**

⑦ **How do you plan to implement these mindsets into your life so that you don't forget to live them?**

Can you set reminders on your phone, hang inspirational quotes that remind you of a particular belief, or practice positive self affirmations? There are several ways to implement the mindsets—what will you do?

## SECTION 2
# GETTING STARTED WITH GOAL SETTING

# The FOCUSED Framework™

*"If you want to be happy, set a goal that commands your thoughts, liberates your energy and inspires your hopes."*

– Andrew Carnegie

## CHAPTER NOTES

Following the previous chapter, how are you feeling? What thoughts are running through your mind? Jot them down here for later reference.

## The FOCUSED Framework™

*Crush Your Goals!*

## The FOCUSED Framework™

**WORKSHEET**

## *The FOCUSED Framework*

☐ **Write one of your goals here:**

_____

_____

### *Is your goal:*

☐ **Future-Focused**
Is this goal going to move me forward and contribute to the future that I envision for myself?

☐ **Optimistic**
Is this goal an optimistic goal that will make a positive change in my life and am I optimistic that I can achieve it?

☐ **Challenging**
Is this goal going to be difficult to achieve and require me to stretch and grow? Am I going to have to push myself?

☐ **Unforgettable**
Am I so passionate about this goal that it's all I can think about? Do I wake up every day excited to work towards it?

☐ **Significant**
Is this goal significant to me and my current place in life? Does it add significance to my life? Is this goal going to take me to a new level?

☐ **Energizing**
Does this goal get me pumped up and energized? Am I excited to pursue it? Does this goal lift my spirit and my attitude?

☐ **Deadline-Driven**
Does my goal have a finite deadline or a milestone that I can reach?

⑦ **Do you have a strong emotional connection to this**

### *The FOCUSED Framework*™

goal? Why or why not?

_____
_____
_____

⑦ **If any of the FOCUSED elements are missing, do you think you still have a good shot at success with this goal? Why or why not?**

Keep in mind that your goals don't have to hit all seven items on The FOCUSED Framework™ checklist.

The more items you can check off, the better chance you have in seeing success with your goal, but falling one item short does not necessarily mean you shouldn't pursue the goal.

_____
_____
_____
_____

⑦ **Overall, how would you rate this goal?**

With 1 being "I don't feel very confident about this goal—it doesn't seem to fit the framework" and 10 being "This goal fits the framework, and I'm going to crush it!"

| 1 | 2 | 3 | 4 | 5 | 6 | 7 | 8 | 9 | 10 |
|---|---|---|---|---|---|---|---|---|----|
|   |   |   |   |   |   |   |   |   |    |

⑦ **Are you going to give yourself a reward for crushing this goal? If so, what will it be?**

_____
_____
_____

**WORKSHEET**

# The FOCUSED Framework

☐ **Write one of your goals here:**

_____

_____

_____

## *Is your goal:*

☐ **Future-Focused**
Is this goal going to move me forward and contribute to the future that I envision for myself?

☐ **Optimistic**
Is this goal an optimistic goal that will make a positive change in my life and am I optimistic that I can achieve it?

☐ **Challenging**
Is this goal going to be difficult to achieve and require me to stretch and grow? Am I going to have to push myself?

☐ **Unforgettable**
Am I so passionate about this goal that it's all I can think about? Do I wake up every day excited to work towards it?

☐ **Significant**
Is this goal significant to me and my current place in life? Does it add significance to my life? Is this goal going to take me to a new level?

☐ **Energizing**
Does this goal get me pumped up and energized? Am I excited to pursue it? Does this goal lift my spirit and my attitude?

☐ **Deadline-Driven**
Does my goal have a finite deadline or a milestone that I can reach?

⑦ **Do you have a strong emotional connection to this**

### The FOCUSED Framework™

goal? Why or why not?

_____
_____
_____
_____

**⑦ If any of the FOCUSED elements are missing, do you think you still have a good shot at success with this goal? Why or why not?**

Keep in mind that your goals don't have to hit all seven items on The FOCUSED Framework™ checklist.

The more items you can check off, the better chance you have in seeing success with your goal, but falling one item short does not necessarily mean you shouldn't pursue the goal.

_____
_____
_____
_____

**⑦ Overall, how would you rate this goal?**

With 1 being "I don't feel very confident about this goal—it doesn't seem to fit the framework" and 10 being, "This goal fits the framework, and I'm going to crush it!"

| 1 | 2 | 3 | 4 | 5 | 6 | 7 | 8 | 9 | 10 |
|---|---|---|---|---|---|---|---|---|----|

**⑦ Are you going to give yourself a reward for crushing this goal? If so, what will it be?**

_____
_____
_____

**WORKSHEET**

## *The FOCUSED Framework*

☐ **Write one of your goals here:**

_____

_____

_____

### *Is your goal:*

☐ **Future-Focused**
Is this goal going to move me forward and contribute to the future that I envision for myself?

☐ **Optimistic**
Is this goal an optimistic goal that will make a positive change in my life and am I optimistic that I can achieve it?

☐ **Challenging**
Is this goal going to be difficult to achieve and require me to stretch and grow? Am I going to have to push myself?

☐ **Unforgettable**
Am I so passionate about this goal that it's all I can think about? Do I wake up every day excited to work towards it?

☐ **Significant**
Is this goal significant to me and my current place in life? Does it add significance to my life? Is this goal going to take me to a new level?

☐ **Energizing**
Does this goal get me pumped up and energized? Am I excited to pursue it? Does this goal lift my spirit and my attitude?

☐ **Deadline-Driven**
Does my goal have a finite deadline or a milestone that I can reach?

⊚ **Do you have a strong emotional connection to this**

## The FOCUSED Framework™

goal? Why or why not?

_____
_____
_____

⑦ **If any of the FOCUSED elements are missing, do you think you still have a good shot at success with this goal? Why or why not?**

Keep in mind that your goals don't have to hit all seven items on The FOCUSED Framework™ checklist.

The more items you can check off, the better chance you have in seeing success with your goal, but falling one item short does not necessarily mean you shouldn't pursue the goal.

_____
_____
_____
_____

⑦ **Overall, how would you rate this goal?**

With 1 being "I don't feel very confident about this goal—it doesn't seem to fit the framework" and 10 being, "This goal fits the framework, and I'm going to crush it!"

| 1 | 2 | 3 | 4 | 5 | 6 | 7 | 8 | 9 | 10 |

⑦ **Are you going to give yourself a reward for crushing this goal? If so, what will it be?**

_____
_____
_____

# Four Universal Goals to Start Setting Today

*"Most people overestimate what they can do in one year and underestimate what they can do in ten years."*

– Bill Gates

*Crush Your Goals!*

**CHAPTER NOTES**

Following the previous chapter, how are you feeling? What thoughts are running through your mind? Jot them down here for later reference.

## Four Universal Goals to Start Setting Today

***Crush Your Goals!***

## *Four Universal Goals to Start Setting Today*

## WORKSHEET

# Plan Your 3- to 5-Year Vision

**⑦ What are some of your proudest accomplishments in life so far?**

I use the word accomplishments loosely. It doesn't have to be something huge, like being the class valedictorian or winning a national competition of some kind. It could be a poem you wrote, a class you did very well in, or even a project you made in shop class.

_____

_____

_____

_____

_____

**⑦ Of your accomplishments, which ones made you most excited? Why?**

_____

_____

_____

_____

_____

**⑦ Could you expand on those accomplishments and take them further? Could you build on them? If so, how?**

_____

_____

_____

_____

_____

## Four Universal Goals to Start Setting Today

### ⑦ What does your life look like in 3-5 years?

Where do you work? Who do you surround yourself with most? Have you started a family? Where do you live? Are you happy? Describe your life as if you were telling a close friend.

### ⑦ If it helps, try practicing Blue-Sky Thinking.

Imagine you had absolutely no limits. You could do anything, be anything, and go anywhere you wanted. What would you do? Where would you go? What would your life look like as a whole? Try journaling your vision of your life here and give yourself some time to dream. Be patient; this isn't an easy exercise, but it will help plan your 3-5 year vision.

_____
_____
_____
_____
_____
_____
_____
_____
_____
_____
_____
_____
_____
_____
_____
_____
_____
_____
_____
_____

**WORKSHEET**

# Plan Your Annual & Quarterly Achievement Goals

**❓ Using your 3-5 year vision, what goals do you need to accomplish in the coming year?**

Depending on when you're reading this, the coming year could be the next 365 days, or it could be whatever is left of this calendar year. It's totally up to you.

1. _____
2. _____
3. _____
4. _____
5. _____
6. _____
7. _____
8. _____
9. _____
10. _____

**❓ Of the goals above, which ones are you going to focus on in this quarter?**

Remember to be selective. Aim for 3-5 goals per quarter across several categories such as personal, fitness, professional, family, spiritual, etc.

1. _____
2. _____
3. _____
4. _____
5. _____

### Four Universal Goals to Start Setting Today

❓ **Rewrite your new quarterly goals below and then write the next 3 actions you need to take for each.**

1. _____
   - ☐ _____
   - ☐ _____
   - ☐ _____
2. _____
   - ☐ _____
   - ☐ _____
   - ☐ _____
3. _____
   - ☐ _____
   - ☐ _____
   - ☐ _____
4. _____
   - ☐ _____
   - ☐ _____
   - ☐ _____
5. _____
   - ☐ _____
   - ☐ _____
   - ☐ _____

↪ Now you have the beginnings of a concrete action plan for the quarter ahead. Be sure to keep expanding on your plan as you progress. Good luck and have fun!

*Crush Your Goals!*

**WORKSHEET**

## Set and Track a Habit Goal

☐ **Write one of your Habit goals here:**

_____

_____

❓ **What motivated you to set this goal?**

Connecting with your intrinsic motivations is a great way to build momentum behind a new habit. List your top three here:

**1.** _____

**2.** _____

**3.** _____

☐ **What reward are you going to give yourself once you've achieved your goal?**

_____

## Track Your Daily Progress

The latest research shows it takes 66 days to build a habit. Track your momentum here and be sure to give yourself a reward at the end.

| 1  | 2  | 3  | 4  | 5  | 6  | 7  | 8  | 9  | 10 | 11 |
|----|----|----|----|----|----|----|----|----|----|----|
| 12 | 13 | 14 | 15 | 16 | 17 | 18 | 19 | 20 | 21 | 22 |
| 23 | 24 | 25 | 26 | 27 | 28 | 29 | 30 | 31 | 32 | 33 |
| 34 | 35 | 36 | 37 | 38 | 39 | 40 | 41 | 42 | 43 | 45 |
| 46 | 47 | 48 | 49 | 50 | 51 | 52 | 53 | 54 | 55 | 56 |
| 57 | 58 | 59 | 60 | 61 | 62 | 63 | 64 | 65 | 66 | Reward |

*Four Universal Goals to Start Setting Today*

**WORKSHEET**

## Set and Track a Habit Goal

☐ **Write one of your Habit goals here:**

_____
_____
_____

⓸ **What motivated you to set this goal?**

Connecting with your intrinsic motivations is a great way to build momentum behind a new habit. List your top three here:

**1.** _____

**2.** _____

**3.** _____

☐ **What reward are you going to give yourself once you've achieved your goal?**

_____
_____

## Track Your Daily Progress

The latest research shows it takes 66 days to build a habit. Track your momentum here and be sure to give yourself a reward at the end.

| 1 | 2 | 3 | 4 | 5 | 6 | 7 | 8 | 9 | 10 | 11 |
|---|---|---|---|---|---|---|---|---|----|----|
| 12 | 13 | 14 | 15 | 16 | 17 | 18 | 19 | 20 | 21 | 22 |
| 23 | 24 | 25 | 26 | 27 | 28 | 29 | 30 | 31 | 32 | 33 |
| 34 | 35 | 36 | 37 | 38 | 39 | 40 | 41 | 42 | 43 | 45 |
| 46 | 47 | 48 | 49 | 50 | 51 | 52 | 53 | 54 | 55 | 56 |
| 57 | 58 | 59 | 60 | 61 | 62 | 63 | 64 | 65 | 66 | Reward |

# Prioritize Like a Pro & Crush Your Goals in Record Time

*"Most of us spend too much time on what is urgent and not enough time on what is important."*

– Stephen R. Covey

**CHAPTER NOTES**

Following the previous chapter, how are you feeling? What thoughts are running through your mind? Jot them down here for later reference.

## *Prioritize Like a Pro*

## *Crush Your Goals!*

## Prioritize Like a Pro

**WORKSHEET**

# The Eisenhower Matrix and the Four Ds

To help identify what's most important on your to-do list, dump all of your tasks and projects into this matrix. I've already added the Four Ds to the matrix for you as well.

Remember, if everything is important, nothing is important. It may help to redraw the matrix on larger paper if you have a large to-do list.

|  | Urgent | Not Urgent |
|---|---|---|
| **Important** | Do It | Defer It |
| **Not Important** | Delegate It | Delete It |

## *Prioritize Like a Pro*

**⑦ Which tasks are you going to do immediately and which are you going to defer? These are your important tasks, or goals, for the foreseeable future.**

| To Do | Defer |
|---|---|
| _____ | _____ |
| _____ | _____ |
| _____ | _____ |
| _____ | _____ |
| _____ | _____ |

**⑦ Which of your tasks are you going to delegate and who are you going to delegate them to?**

| Task | Delegate |
|---|---|
| _____ | _____ |
| _____ | _____ |
| _____ | _____ |
| _____ | _____ |
| _____ | _____ |

**⑦ Which of your tasks are you going to delete?**

It may help to also list the reason for deletion to help achieve closure. Is the task no longer important to your mission? Was it ever important? Has someone else already done it?

_____
_____
_____
_____

**WORKSHEET**

# Getting Started with Time Blocking

❓ **Time Blocking is the practice of scheduling blocks of time in advance to help complete your top priority tasks without interruption. To get started, list out all of your important tasks and projects.**

To help identify what's most important, refer to the Eisenhower matrix on the previous worksheet.

1. _____
2. _____
3. _____
4. _____
5. _____
6. _____
7. _____
8. _____
9. _____
10. _____

❓ **Next, which method of time blocking are you going to try first?**

The Pomodoro Technique consists of 25-minute blocks with a short break, but you could also try 50-minute blocks with a 10-minute break, 90-minute blocks with a longer break, or whatever works best for you. Describe the time blocking method you're going to try here:

_____
_____
_____
_____

Before we dive into time blocking our tasks and projects, let's make time for email, appointments, meetings, task management, and so on.

- **Open your preferred calendar, whether it's analog or digital, and set one or two daily blocks for email and task management.**

    It helps to set this as a recurring event at the same time each day to develop and reinforce the habit. I plan one of these blocks in the morning and another in the late afternoon.

- **Next, ensure that all of your current meetings and appointments are already on your calendar.**

    Going forward, meetings will become secondary to your existing time blocks, but for now, it's okay to block off the meetings that you already have. Once you get into a rhythm of time blocking, the gaps between your blocks will become time slots for meetings and appointments.

- **Finally, begin scheduling your projects and tasks within the time blocks of your choosing.**

    Be sure to leave some breathing room for additional meetings or spontaneous appointments that may pop up. I like to set two daily blocks for email and task management and three daily blocks for my top-level projects, totaling five 50-minute blocks. That leaves two to three blocks for meetings each day.

## Here are some other tips and tricks for time blocking to keep in mind:

- If you need to free up space on a particular day, you can move blocks as needed, but don't delete blocks unless the task or project is no longer important.
- Only move time blocks when it serves an important purpose—don't get in the habit of allowing everyone else's priorities bump your own. Defend your time blocks.

**WORKSHEET**

## *Prioritize Like a Pro: Pareto's Principle*

**Pareto's Principle** states that, for many events, roughly 80% of the effects come from 20% of the causes. In other words, 20% of what you're doing contributes to 80% of your success. The other 80% might be a waste of your time.

**List a few of the goals that you hope to achieve in the next 60-90 days:**

1. _____
2. _____
3. _____
4. _____
5. _____

**Now, which of the tasks and actions are the 20% of tasks and actions that will have the greatest impact on helping you achieve these goals?**

> These have a huge impact on your success and are typically best performed by you. For example, on my blog, it's best if I write the articles, but someone else could create the social media graphics and share the final article.

_____
_____
_____
_____
_____
_____
_____

***Prioritize Like a Pro***

- ⓘ **Next, which of the tasks and actions are the 80% of tasks and actions that will have the smallest impact on helping you achieve these goals?**

    These typically require a great deal of your time and energy, contribute very little to your success, and can often be delegated or outsourced. For me, selecting stock images, creating graphics, posting to social, building email campaigns, and so on aren't as crucial as creating the original content for my blog.

    _____
    _____
    _____
    _____
    _____
    _____
    _____
    _____
    _____

- ⓘ **Looking at these two lists, how can you spend more time doing the 20% while spending less time doing the 80%? What plan can you develop to focus on the 20%?**

    For example, I decided to hire a part-time intern to help me create social graphics, post to social media, and create my email campaigns.

    _____
    _____
    _____
    _____
    _____
    _____
    _____

**WORKSHEET**

## *Implementing The ABCDE Method*

The **ABCDE Method of Prioritization** is a filter similar to the Four Ds. However, the ABCDE Method helps prioritize your tasks by grading them with a letter.

- **Using the following page, write down all of your current tasks and projects and then grade them using the key below.**

    **A**—These tasks are critical and have high consequences. Getting them done should be your top priority because these tasks contribute the most to your long-term success.

    **B**—These tasks have smaller consequences, though they are still important, such as answering email.

    **C**—These tasks would be good to do, but they have no consequence on your life at all. Nothing terrible will happen if these items are never completed.

    **D**—"D" is for Delegate. These are the tasks that should be done by someone else so that you can focus on the big picture.

    **E**—"E" is for Eliminate. These tasks are not worth doing at all by anyone.

- **Once you're done grading your tasks and projects, schedule time to complete your top-level goals.**
- **Then, reach out to your colleagues or your employees and ask them to take on your D-level tasks.**
- **Be sure to get closure on your E-level tasks so that they don't continue to drain your energy.**

## *Prioritize Like a Pro*

Grade    Task

# The Best Tools for Tracking Your Goals

*"All the tools, techniques and technology in the world are nothing without the head, heart and hands to use them wisely, kindly and mindfully."*

– Rasheed Ogunlaru

**CHAPTER NOTES**

Following the previous chapter, how are you feeling? What thoughts are running through your mind? Jot them down here for later reference.

## The Best Tools for Tracking Your Goals

*Crush Your Goals!*

## The Best Tools for Tracking Your Goals

**WORKSHEET**

## The Best Tools for Tracking Your Goals

For your convenience, I wanted to provide a list of tracker types and examples to get your brainstorming started:

- **Journals and Planners**
  Michael Hyatt's Full Focus Planner
  Brendon Burchard's High Performance Planner
  90X Goal Planner

- **Specific Apps for Data-Driven Goals**
  BodySpace for weight lifting
  Strava for running and cycling
  MyFitnessPal for calorie counting
  Daily Water Tracker Reminder for water intake

- **Interactive Scoreboard**
  Whiteboard, Chalkboard, or Cork board
  Year-at-a-Glance Calendar

- **Analog or Digital Calendar**
  Microsoft Outlook
  Apple Calendar
  Google Calendar

**Which tracking tools have you tried in the past? Did they work? Why or why not?**

> For example, I've tried apps that remind me of my goals in the past, but they failed because I personally ignore notifications. I've also tried notebooks in the past that failed due to a lack of guidance and structure.

_____
_____
_____
_____
_____
_____

## The Best Tools for Tracking Your Goals

**② Write down the goals you want to track and which type of tracker you're going to try:**

Goal                                    Tracker

_____                 _____
_____                 _____
_____                 _____
_____                 _____
_____                 _____


**② How are you going to ensure that each tracker is successful? How will you evaluate each tracker?**

For example, I'm going to track all of my top-level goals in my Full Focus Planner, and I'll use a year-at-a-glance calendar to ensure I review my planner daily. The calendar will be my interactive scoreboard.

I'm also going to track my daily water intake using an app, but I will list my water intake goal in my Full Focus Planner. Then, I will review my water intake every Sunday as part of my weekly review, ensuring that the app is working.

**What's your plan?**

_____
_____
_____
_____
_____
_____
_____
_____
_____
_____

## SECTION 3
# ESTABLISHING A SYSTEM FOR SUCCESS

# Assemble a Support Team

*"If you want to go fast, go alone. If you want to go far, go together."*

– African Proverb

**CHAPTER NOTES**

Following the previous chapter, how are you feeling? What thoughts are running through your mind? Jot them down here for later reference.

## *Assemble a Support Team*

*Crush Your Goals!*

## *Assemble a Support Team*

**WORKSHEET**

## *Establish an Accountability Partnership*

⑦ **Has there been a time in your life that you've had an accountability partner for a goal or resolution? Did it work out? Why or why not? If not, where did it go wrong?**

_____

_____

_____

_____

_____

_____

_____

_____

_____

⑦ **Can you create a list of your current goals and the traits that a good accountability partner might need? Pretend you're writing a want ad. What would it say?**

For example, to achieve my half-marathon goal, I want to run several times per week before work. I would need an accountability partner who either loves to run in the mornings or is also training for a half-marathon in the mornings. It would help if this person was also male and runs a similar pace to me (9:15 minutes/mile).

☐ **Goal 1:**

_____

_____

_____

_____

### Assemble a Support Team

☐ **Goal 2:**

_____
_____
_____
_____
_____

☐ **Goal 3:**

_____
_____
_____
_____
_____

⑦ **Using the descriptions above, do you have people in your life who you trust and respect and that might be interested in pursuing an accountability partnership? If so, write them here:**

_____
_____
_____
_____

**Before you rush into anything, remember these guidelines:**

- ✓ An accountability partnership is meant to be supportive, not combative. It's a partnership.
- ✓ It's better to take your time and pick an ideal person than it is to approach someone hastily and then need to break things off, especially when approaching a friend or family member.

**WORKSHEET**

## *Joining or Starting a Mastermind Group*

❓ **To get started with a Mastermind group, the first thing to ask is, are there any groups already formed in your area? Who could you ask? Make a list of contacts and reach out to each of them and ask if they know of any groups.**

Don't worry; you're not committing to anything yet—you're just asking if any groups exist.

☐ _____
☐ _____
☐ _____
☐ _____
☐ _____

❓ **Did you find any groups or additional contacts to call? If so, write them below. If not, proceed to the next page.**

☐ _____
☐ _____
☐ _____

👉 **After finding a group or two, reach out and ask if you can come to an informational or introductory meeting. The purpose is to get a feel of the group mission, member dynamics, and so on.**

**Go into the first meeting thinking, "Is this a group or people I would want to spend a year or more with?"**

A Mastermind group is a commitment. Don't join just to join. Be sure that your goals for the group are congruent with the goals and mission of the group you're visiting. For example, some groups share wisdom and support, some exchange business contacts and leads, some focus on goals and high performance, and so on. Avoid joining a group that doesn't align with your needs.

**Assemble a Support Team**

## Starting a Mastermind Group

Assuming you couldn't find a group to join, or couldn't find a group that aligned with your needs, you might want to start your own group.

- **What is the mission, vision, and focus for the group you want to start?**

    Example: Bringing together a tight knit group of high-performing individuals to encourage and support one another through our individual expertise, feedback, networking, and accountability. We aim to hold each other accountable to the goals that we set for ourselves and we're always looking for ways to add value, share wisdom within the group, and help one another grow.

    _____
    _____
    _____
    _____
    _____
    _____

- **List several individuals you think might be interested in joining, and then follow the steps below.**

    _____      _____
    _____      _____
    _____      _____

1. **Set up a preliminary meeting to align your visions, discuss a meeting format, and schedule a recurring meeting time.**
2. **Start a Facebook group and document your mission, vision, group guidelines, and meeting times.**
3. **Meet regularly and adjust the format as needed. It's okay if things evolve as time goes on.**

**WORKSHEET**

## *Finding a Mentor*

⑦ **Before seeking a mentor, it's crucial to establish why you want or need a mentor. Do you want general guidance, career advice, help with a specific goal, or something else? Spend a few minutes and write out what you're hoping to receive from a mentorship. How do you hope to grow?**

_____

_____

_____

_____

_____

⑦ **Given your goals, make a list of a few people that you could ask to be your mentor. Try not to be intimidated to write down prominent people from your community.**

If you're unsure of who could help mentor you around your specific goals, use this space to identify a few people you could ask for help. Your boss, your friends, and your social networks are great places to start asking, "Do you know who could help mentor me to do _____."

Check each person off your list as you reach out to them.

☐ _____

☐ _____

☐ _____

☐ _____

☞ **Once you identify someone in your community that you would like to have as a mentor, ask if you can buy them lunch. Make it clear that it's not a sales meeting and that you only want to meet to get acquainted.**

## Assemble a Support Team

👉 **Over lunch, keep the following talking points, tasks, and guidelines in mind:**

1. Get to know him or her a little better. Ask them about their life, their businesses, and their success.
2. Share a little about yourself as well. Tell them about your goals and aspirations.
3. Explain your motivations for wanting to achieve success and how you admire what they've done in your shared industry.
4. Many times, once a prospective mentor sees your common interest and goals, they will offer up their advice, but if they don't, just ask them for their opinion.
5. Then ask if it would be okay to reach out again in the future if you have any other questions.
6. Finally, pay the bill and go your separate ways. **Don't ask this person to be your mentor on the spot. You wouldn't ask a person to marry you on the first date, so don't ask for a formal mentorship over the first lunch.**

👉 **As time goes on, reach out to the person a time or two and then gently ask if he or she would be willing to mentor you in your area of interest.**

Let he or she know that you're serious about your success, and you don't want to waste their time. Make it known that you would value their time and guidance and would work hard to return the favor.

👉 **If they agree, ask about how they would like to conduct the mentorship.**

How long are they willing to help? Three months? A Year? Indefinitely? How often do they want to meet and for how long? Is it okay to text and call, or should you stick to email only? Work out the logistics so that it's easier on your mentor, even if it's a little more difficult for you.

👉 **Once you nail down the logistics of the mentorship, give the relationship your best effort and try to do everything that your mentor asks you to do.**

You may not agree with everything your mentor says, and that's okay. However, remember that you asked them to coach you for a reason, so don't dismiss his or her ideas too quickly. Your new mentor is investing time and energy in you. This is time and energy that they could be spending on countless other things, so make it count and do your absolute best.

# The Four Cs of High-Performance Goal Setting

*"If we practice being spectacular long enough, spectacular will become our way of being."*

– Robin Sharma

**CHAPTER NOTES**

Following the previous chapter, how are you feeling? What thoughts are running through your mind? Jot them down here for later reference.

## *The Four Cs of High Performance Goal Setting*

**Crush Your Goals!**

## The Four Cs of High Performance Goal Setting

**WORKSHEET**

# *The Four Cs of High Performance*

The best way to get started with the Four Cs is to reflect on your recent past and your present and think through each of the Four Cs. This worksheet will guide you through the process.

⑦ **Let's start with Completion. In your recent past or your present, write out some of your biggest wins, proudest moments, or successful goals.**

Dig deep and don't hold back. If it was an achievement, a goal your crushed, or something that made you feel good, write it down.

_____

_____

_____

_____

_____

⑦ **Of the items above, did you allow yourself to feel the win, or did you quickly dismiss your accomplishment and move on to the next thing? Take a second to feel your win and bask in your success. How do you feel?**

Remember, when we see a goal through to 100% completion, we receive a surge of endorphins that make us feel good. It's okay to soak up that feeling and celebrate your success.

_____

_____

_____

_____

_____

## The Four Cs of High Performance Goal Setting

⑦ **Next, let's find some Closure. In your recent past or your present, have there been any goals you've abandoned or decided to not follow through with? List those here:**

Remember, if a goal is 99% done, it's not done. To feel the success, endorphins, and sense of closure, a goal needs to be 100% complete.

_____
_____
_____
_____
_____
_____

⑦ **In order to find Closure for these abandoned goals, and to cut loose the Energy Anchors you've potentially created, identify why you've stopped pursuing the goal and craft a plan for moving forward.**

Did you decide the goal was the wrong goal? Why or why not? Did you quit when the goal became too difficult? Can you connect it with a stronger *why* and reboot the goal? Was the timing wrong? Could you save the goal for later and circle back to it? Write out your reasoning and your plan for Closure below.

_____
_____
_____
_____
_____
_____
_____
_____
_____
_____
_____
_____

*Crush Your Goals!*

⑦ Now that we've celebrated some of our successes and cut ties with our Energy Anchors, let's renew our Commitments. Make a list of the goals you're actively pursuing or wish to pursue.

1. _____
2. _____
3. _____
4. _____
5. _____
6. _____
7. _____
8. _____

It's easy to believe that we've committed to a goal until we take a hard look at what commitment means. To be fully committed to the goals above, you would ideally answer "yes" to all of the questions below.

⑦ I am 100% committed to each goal AND to the effort, focus, discipline, and time it will take to crush it.

☐ Yes ☐ No

⑦ I have a zero-tolerance policy against excuses.

☐ Yes ☐ No

⑦ I will decline any activity that might derail my goals because my goals are unbreakable commitments.

☐ Yes ☐ No

⑦ Life-changing goals are challenging, but I'm committed to the challenge and will not stop until I'm 100% complete.

☐ Yes ☐ No

## The Four Cs of High Performance Goal Setting

⑦ **Of the goals you're now committed to, are there any goals that will compete for your time, energy, resources, or focus?**

For example, are you planning a home renovation while also training for a half-marathon? Do you have enough time and energy to do both without succumbing to total exhaustion? Are you planning to write a blog post each week while simultaneously writing a book? Is that possible? These were competing goals I've personally had to address and overcome. What about you?

**Are any of your goals in competition? If so, how will to plan to overcome it?**

_____
_____
_____
_____
_____
_____
_____
_____
_____

⑦ **If needed, put some of your competing goals in a backlog for a later date. Just because a goal is important doesn't mean you have to do it right now. Which goals will you save for later?**

1. _____
2. _____
3. _____
4. _____
5. _____

# Develop a Daily, Success-Driven Routine

*"You will never change your life until you change something you do daily. The secret of your success is found in your daily routine."*

– John C. Maxwell

**CHAPTER NOTES**

Following the previous chapter, how are you feeling? What thoughts are running through your mind? Jot them down here for later reference.

## *Develop a Daily, Success-Driven Routine*

**Crush Your Goals!**

**Develop a Daily, Success-Driven Routine**

**WORKSHEET**

## *Developing a Success-Driven Routine*

Our daily habits and actions are directly connected to our future outcomes. That's why most good routines are built around our long-term goals—we begin with the end in mind.

⑦ **What long-term goals are you planning to crush using a daily routine?**

1. _____
2. _____
3. _____
4. _____
5. _____

⑦ **How can you break your long-term goals down into manageable, daily or weekly actions? You might want to focus on one long-term goal at a time and repeat this exercise as needed, but oftentimes goals can work to support one another.**

> For example, in order to publish this book, I had to carve our time to write, edit, and re-write every day. To run my first half-marathon, I had to run, stretch, and eat properly every week. My morning routine works towards all of my goals. What tasks and actions move you closer to your long-term goals?

1. _____
2. _____
3. _____
4. _____
5. _____
6. _____
7. _____

## *Develop a Daily, Success-Driven Routine*

⑦ **Next, how might you combine or schedule your new actions and tasks into a daily routine that supports your goals?**

For example, I wake up at 4 a.m. and start my morning with some French-pressed coffee. At 4:15, I dive into my projects, whether it's writing my book, working on my blog, or some other project. Then, at 7 a.m., I gather my things, blend my post-workout smoothie, and go to the gym where I either lift or run while listening to an audio book. I end with some time in the sauna, a shower, and then I go to work at 9 a.m.

After the workday and my evening at home, I lay out my clothes for the next day and go to bed no later than 9:30 p.m. Depending on the day, I might do some light reading in bed.

| Time | Task |
| --- | --- |
| _____ | _____ |
| _____ | _____ |
| _____ | _____ |
| _____ | _____ |
| _____ | _____ |
| _____ | _____ |
| _____ | _____ |
| _____ | _____ |

⑦ **In reviewing your new routine, does it support the goals outlined on the previous page?**

☐ Yes ☐ No

⑦ **If not, how can you fix or modify it? Make your changes above.**

⑦ **Looking at the routine, are you confident that you can stick to it?**

Remember, habits and routines are connected, and habits take time to build, maybe even 66 days or more. Don't forget to think about your *why*.

☐ Yes ☐ No

# Build Momentum Using the Domino Effect

*"It does not matter how slowly you go as long as you do not stop."*

– Confucius

## CHAPTER NOTES

Following the previous chapter, how are you feeling? What thoughts are running through your mind? Jot them down here for later reference.

## Build Momentum Using the Domino Effect

**Crush Your Goals!**

## Build Momentum Using the Domino Effect

**WORKSHEET**

## Build Momentum Using the Domino Effect

⑦ **What is one of your biggest FOCUSED Goals?**

_____
_____


⑦ **Using the following lines, write down as many tasks and milestones as you can think of that must happen for your goal to be a success.**

Don't worry about prioritizing them just yet. Just let the ideas flow.

_____
_____
_____
_____
_____
_____
_____
_____
_____
_____
_____
_____
_____

## Build Momentum Using the Domino Effect

⑦ Now, using the numbered lines below, sort your tasks by priority and place them in sequential order. What has to be done first? Second? Third?

# These are your new domino goals.

1. _____
2. _____
3. _____
4. _____
5. _____
6. _____
7. _____
8. _____
9. _____
10. _____
11. _____
12. _____
13. _____
14. _____
15. _____
16. _____
17. _____
18. _____

↪ Finally, transfer your new domino goals to your calendar, whiteboard, or notebook; give each of them a hard deadline; and watch your momentum build as you crush your goals!

# SECTION 4
# DEALING WITH DIFFICULTIES

# How to Stay Motivated

*"You didn't lose your motivation, you just forgot what you're fighting for."*

– Brendon Burchard

## CHAPTER NOTES

Following the previous chapter, how are you feeling? What thoughts are running through your mind? Jot them down here for later reference.

## How to Stay Motivated

*Crush Your Goals!*

## How to Stay Motivated

*Crush Your Goals!*

**WORKSHEET**

## *Getting Motivated to Crush Your Goals*

This worksheet was designed to help you find your motivations for pursuing a goal, but it's also possible that the goal is the problem, not your motivations. We'll explore both sides of the equation here.

☐ **Write one of your goals that you're struggling with here:**

_____
_____
_____

⊙ **Overall, how motivated are you to crush this goal?**

With 1 being "I don't feel very motivated towards this goal—at all" and 10 being "I'm pumped about this goal! I'm motivated and I can't wait to crush it!"

| 1 | 2 | 3 | 4 | 5 | 6 | 7 | 8 | 9 | 10 |
|---|---|---|---|---|---|---|---|---|----|

⊙ **What originally motivated you to set this goal?**

Did it just sound good at the time? Were other people doing it, so you jumped on the bandwagon? Or did you have a strong *why* for this goal? If so, what was your *why*?

_____
_____
_____
_____
_____
_____
_____

## *How to Stay Motivated*

⑦ **Is that motivation still driving you? Why or why not?**

Are you motivated to pursue something else or do you need a stronger motivation, or *why*, to keep pursuing this goal?

⑦ **If you plan to keep pursuing this goal, have your motivations changed or deepened? How so?**

⑦ **Or have you decided to abandon this goal?**

If you plan to ditch this goal be sure to find closure and avoid creating Energy Anchors. It's okay to abandon a goal as long as you have a reason that you feel good about. What's your reason for moving on?

⑦ **If you're ditching this goal, are you going to replace it with a new goal? If so, you might consider revisiting the Discover and Embrace Your *Why* or The FOCUSED Framework worksheets to get started on the right foot.**

## WORKSHEET

# *Getting Motivated to Crush Your Goals*

This worksheet was designed to help you find your motivations for pursuing a goal, but it's also possible that the goal is the problem, not your motivations. We'll explore both sides of the equation here.

☐ **Write one of your goals that you're struggling with here:**

___

### Overall, how motivated are you to crush this goal?

With 1 being "I don't feel very motivated towards this goal—at all" and 10 being "I'm pumped about this goal! I'm motivated and I can't wait to crush it!"

| 1 | 2 | 3 | 4 | 5 | 6 | 7 | 8 | 9 | 10 |
|---|---|---|---|---|---|---|---|---|----|

### What originally motivated you to set this goal?

Did it just sound good at the time? Were other people doing it, so you jumped on the bandwagon? Or did you have a strong *why* for this goal? If so, what was your *why*?

___

## *How to Stay Motivated*

⑦ **Is that motivation still driving you? Why or why not?**

Are you motivated to pursue something else or do you need a stronger motivation, or *why*, to keep pursuing this goal?

_____
_____
_____
_____
_____

⑦ **If you plan to keep pursuing this goal, have your motivations changed or deepened? How so?**

_____
_____
_____
_____
_____

⑦ **Or have you decided to abandon this goal?**

If you plan to ditch this goal be sure to find closure and avoid creating Energy Anchors. It's okay to abandon a goal as long as you have a reason that you feel good about. What's your reason for moving on?

_____
_____
_____
_____
_____

⑦ **If you're ditching this goal, are you going to replace it with a new goal? If so, you might consider revisiting the Discover and Embrace Your *Why* or The FOCUSED Framework worksheets to get started on the right foot.**

**WORKSHEET**

# Getting Motivated to Crush Your Goals

This worksheet was designed to help you find your motivations for pursuing a goal, but it's also possible that the goal is the problem, not your motivations. We'll explore both sides of the equation here.

☐ **Write one of your goals that you're struggling with here:**

_____
_____
_____

❓ **Overall, how motivated are you to crush this goal?**

With 1 being "I don't feel very motivated towards this goal—at all" and 10 being "I'm pumped about this goal! I'm motivated and I can't wait to crush it!"

| 1 | 2 | 3 | 4 | 5 | 6 | 7 | 8 | 9 | 10 |
|---|---|---|---|---|---|---|---|---|----|

❓ **What originally motivated you to set this goal?**

Did it just sound good at the time? Were other people doing it, so you jumped on the bandwagon? Or did you have a strong *why* for this goal? If so, what was your *why*?

_____
_____
_____
_____
_____
_____
_____

## How to Stay Motivated

- **Is that motivation still driving you? Why or why not?**

    Are you motivated to pursue something else or do you need a stronger motivation, or *why*, to keep pursuing this goal?

- **If you plan to keep pursuing this goal, have your motivations changed or deepened? How so?**

- **Or have you decided to abandon this goal?**

    If you plan to ditch this goal be sure to find closure and avoid creating Energy Anchors. It's okay to abandon a goal as long as you have a reason that you feel good about. What's your reason for moving on?

- **If you're ditching this goal, are you going to replace it with a new goal? If so, you might consider revisiting the Discover and Embrace Your *Why or* The FOCUSED Framework worksheets to get started on the right foot.**

# Five Tips for Overcoming Obstacles

"Challenges are gifts that force us to search for a new center of gravity. Don't fight them, just find a new way to stand."

– Oprah Winfrey

## CHAPTER NOTES

Following the previous chapter, how are you feeling? What thoughts are running through your mind? Jot them down here for later reference.

## Five Tips for Overcoming Obstacles

## *Crush Your Goals!*

## *Five Tips for Overcoming Obstacles*

**WORKSHEET**

## *Overcoming Obstacles and Setbacks*

Teaching people how to overcome obstacles can be challenging. Everyone's situations are uniquely different and vary in severity. You may have already overcome a multitude of obstacles in your life. You may be experiencing a rough patch right now as you read this. Or it may be blue skies and smooth sailing. Either way, setbacks in life are inevitable at some point.

To apply each strategy from the chapter, I'm going to ask you to either reflect on an old obstacle, think about a current challenge, or plan for a potential future setback. Each question will help you to apply the lessons from the chapter.

> **Thinking about one of your current goals or ambitions, how can you plan for the worst and hope for the best?**

> Here's a personal example: Someday I want to speak on a stage in front 10,000 people. What would I do if I forgot my entire message halfway through? How could I plan to overcome that obstacle? I would most likely take note cards and a small tablet loaded with my talking points, each as a backup to the other. If I were to go blank, I would pause, get a drink of water, and check the timer. All the while I would be calmly checking my notes in an effort to regroup. How can you plan for the worst case scenario?

_____

_____

_____

_____

_____

_____

_____

## *Five Tips for Overcoming Obstacles*

⑦ **Thinking about a past or future disappointment, what plan or strategies can you put in place to limit your disappointment and allow yourself to move on more quickly?**

You may recall these examples from the chapter:

Call a friend or mentor and talk it through with them. Get some outside perspective on your situation. Often times, talking about the problem out loud will help you accept it and move on more quickly.

Time block your dwelling by allowing yourself to dwell for no more than one hour.

Give yourself a pep talk. Tell yourself that you need to move on, that you're human, and you're allowed to make mistakes or experience setbacks.

If all else fails, find a way to distract yourself until you can calm down and reexamine things with a clear mind.

What will your plan be?

_____
_____
_____
_____
_____
_____
_____
_____
_____
_____

⑦ **Imagine one of the biggest failures from your past and write it down below. Then, reflect deeply and think about a lesson you can learn from that perceived failure.**

There's a lesson in everything, so don't move on until you come up with something positive. Doing this exercise now will help you think through future setbacks as they occur.

## *Crush Your Goals!*

⑦ **Think about a goal that has or is currently frustrating you. Maybe you fell short of your goal. Perhaps it's taking way longer than you thought it would. Maybe it's far more difficult than you ever imagined.**

**Now, apply the Better Every Day Mindset to the goal. Where would you be or what would life be like if you weren't trying at all?**

For example, maybe you're trying to save money for a vacation but emergencies continue to pop up and deplete your savings. What would happen if you didn't have that savings? Perhaps you're trying to lose 50 pounds and you're stuck at 30. Where would you be had you not tried at all? How is your frustrating goal making you Better Every Day?

### Five Tips for Overcoming Obstacles

⑦ Think about a past goal or situation that presented a seemingly impossible obstacle to you, but because you didn't quit, you miraculously overcame it.

How did you do it? Did you have a choice? You didn't fail because you kept trying, right? You only fail when you quit.

Use the space below to journal about the experience you're thinking about and how you might apply that mindset to future obstacles.

# Moving Beyond Failure

*"Failure is so important. We speak about success all the time. It is the ability to resist failure or use failure that often leads to greater success."*

– J.K. Rowling

## CHAPTER NOTES

Following the previous chapter, how are you feeling? What thoughts are running through your mind? Jot them down here for later reference.

## Moving Beyond Failure

*Crush Your Goals!*

## Moving Beyond Failure

**WORKSHEET**

## *Moving Beyond Failure*

⑦ Many people attempt to avoid failure by not taking any action towards their goals or dreams. Do you believe that not trying is a greater failure than trying and missing the mark? Why or why not?

_____
_____
_____
_____

⑦ If obstacles are the frightful things you see when you take your eyes off of your goals, how will you ensure that you will stay focused on your goals and not the potential for failure?

_____
_____
_____
_____

⑦ Think about some of the things you're currently worried about. Maybe you're worried about losing your job, failing to start your new business, losing money on a bad investment, or something else entirely.

We all have worries. On the following page, make a list of all of your worries. Divide them into two columns: the worries that you could do something about and the worries that are beyond your control.

## *Moving Beyond Failure*

A: Worries you can do something about:

B: Worries that are beyond your control:

⑦ **Next, outline a plan for how you're going to take control of the worries in column A. Things may still not go your way, but if you do everything you can to influence a positive outcome, you will be able to rest easy knowing you did all you could.**

- It may be difficult at first, but if you have worries that are beyond your control (column B), you need to try to forget about them. There's nothing you can do to influence a positive outcome, right?

  What would you tell a friend who shared the same worry that you're suffering with now?

  _____
  _____
  _____
  _____
  _____
  _____

- Think about a perceived failure in your life, either from your distant or very recent past. How was that experience a First Attempt in Learning?

  _____
  _____
  _____
  _____
  _____
  _____

- When we learn from failure and apply the lesson to our next attempt, we improve our chances of success—we fail forward. What are some ways that you've failed forward in the past?

  _____
  _____

*Moving Beyond Failure*

⑦ **There is no shortcut or elevator to success; you have to take the stairs. As we overcome failure, we build upon failure. Each failure that we overcome becomes a step in our success staircase.**

Think about where you are today. What past failures have helped you get to where you are today?

⑦ **Having reflected on you past failures, how you've overcome them, and how they've contributed to your current success, is there really any point in fearing potential future failure? Why or why not?**

# 16
# Take Action Today!

*"The path to success is to take massive, determined actions."*

– Tony Robbins

## CHAPTER NOTES

Following the previous chapter, how are you feeling? What thoughts are running through your mind? Jot them down here for later reference.

## Take Action Today!

***Crush Your Goals!***

## Take Action Today!

**WORKSHEET**

# Taking Massive Action!

**① Overall, how do you feel about jumping in and taking action towards your biggest goals?**

With 1 being "I don't feel very confident, maybe I need to learn more," and 10 being "I'm pumped and I'm ready to take action and crush my goals!"

| 1 | 2 | 3 | 4 | 5 | 6 | 7 | 8 | 9 | 10 |
|---|---|---|---|---|---|---|---|---|----|
|   |   |   |   |   |   |   |   |   |    |

**① If you rated yourself on the lower side, what is holding you back or giving you pause?**

If you rated yourself on the higher side of the scale, what are you waiting for? Use the space on the next page to plan out your next steps.

_____
_____
_____
_____
_____

**① Of the things holding you back, are you willing to take action anyway and risk learning or overcoming them along the way? Why or why not?**

_____
_____
_____
_____
_____
_____

## *Take Action Today!*

? **What if in spite of your lack of confidence you took action anyway? What do you think would happen? What do you have to lose?**

_____
_____
_____
_____
_____

? **What is your biggest FOCUSED Goal?**

_____
_____

? **What are the steps you're going to take to put this goal in motion? What is your battle plan?**

1. _____
2. _____
3. _____
4. _____
5. _____
6. _____
7. _____
8. _____
9. _____
10. _____
11. _____

# About the Author

Austin Bollinger is an entrepreneur, coach, and the founder of Daily New Year's, a blog and podcast dedicated to helping people tap into their true potential and achieve success in every area of their lives.

Austin has a deep-seated passion for helping people overcome fear, self-limiting beliefs, doubt, lack of clarity, and low self-confidence. He is on a mission to build a community of Goal Getters—a group of people who are focused on becoming Better Every Day and living life to the fullest. He aims inspire people around the world to overcome their fears and take massive action towards their dreams every day, not just for a few weeks at the beginning of each year.

Austin lives in Missouri with his best friend and high school sweetheart, Callie, and their two dogs, Rosie and Lily. He is the President of B&B Media is looking forward to authoring several more books in the future.

Meet him at austinbollinger.com.

# Goal Getters, Stay in Touch!

## AUSTINBOLLINGER.COM

✉ austin@dailynewyears.com

◉ @austinjbollinger

🐦 @austinbollinger

in linkedin.com/in/austinjbollinger

f facebook.com/austinjbollinger

## Next Steps

- **Visit** www.crushyourgoalsbook.com for additional copies of the worksheets and for additional resources.
- **Engage** and get plugged into the Daily New Year's community at www.dailynewyears.com.
- **Connect** with Austin at www.austinbollinger.com or on social media.
- **Leave a review** on Amazon or Goodreads to let others know what you thought of the book.

# Work With Austin

*Coaching, Workshops, and More.*

Austin has a deep seated passion for helping people break free of the things that are holding them back so that they can tap into their true potential and step into their dream lives. We all suffer from things like fear, self-limiting beliefs, doubt, lack of clarity, focus, confidence, or direction—but we don't have to face these things alone.

Austin is available for one-on-one coaching sessions and hands-on workshops and trainings. Through coaching, Austin can help you discover a clear path forward and can help you overcome the obstacles that are standing in your way.

Customized, in-person trainings and workshops are a great way to help teams and groups put the strategies from this book into everyday practice. Get in touch and talk to Austin about booking a training today.

www.austinbollinger.com/work-with-me.

# Enjoy This Book?

*Consider sharing it with others!*

- ⊘ Share or mention the book on your social media platforms. Use the hashtag **#CrushYourGoals**.

- ⊘ Write a book review on your blog or on a retailer site.

- ⊘ Pick up a copy for friends, family, coworkers, or anyone who you think would enjoy and be challenged by its message.

- ⊘ Share this message on Twitter, Facebook, or Instagram: **I loved #CrushYourGoals by @AustinJBollinger. Get your copy at crushyourgoalsbook.com.**

- ⊘ Recommend this book for your workplace, book club, class, or friend group.

www.ingramcontent.com/pod-product-compliance
Lightning Source LLC
Chambersburg PA
CBHW071343080526
44587CB00017B/2941